Saving Water and Energy

Heather Hammonds

Contents

Chapter 1

Our Homes

Every day we use water and **energy** in our homes to help us live, work, and play.

We use water for drinking, for washing, and for watering the garden.

We use energy to keep our homes cool or warm, to cook, and to run lots of different machines.

Electricity is a kind of energy. Electricity is used to operate many machines in the home.

Chapter 2

Saving Water

It is important to save water.

Most of our water comes from rivers or lakes. Rivers and lakes fill up when it rains. When it does not rain, there is not as much water.

Dams can be built to trap river water in man-made lakes.

dam

river

Man-made lakes are called reservoirs. Reservoirs store water for people to use.

4

You can help save water!

- Turn off dripping faucets.
- Take short showers.
- Don't leave the faucet running when brushing your teeth.

Water Use

- outdoor
- toilet
- bathroom
- laundry
- kitchen

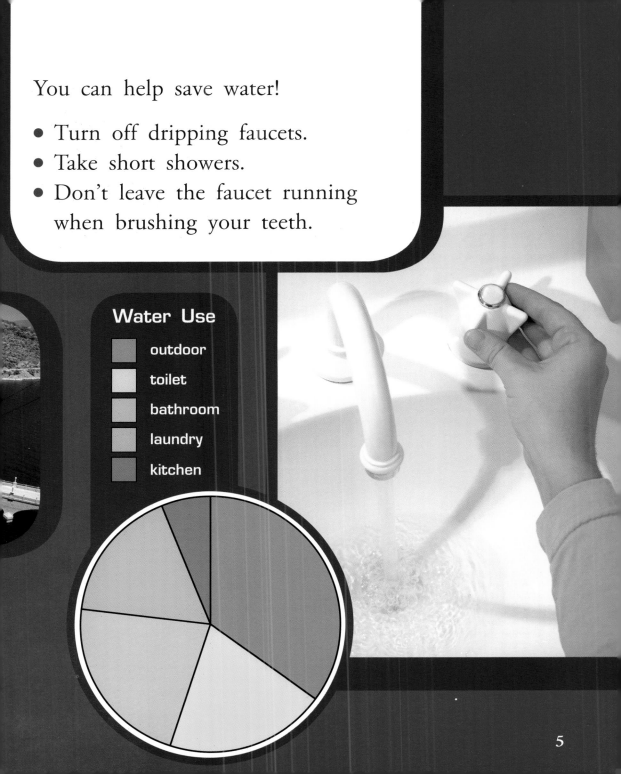

Rainwater Tanks

Some homes do not get water from a river or lake.

This farmhouse has a big **rainwater tank**. The tank can hold lots of water.

When rain falls, it runs off the roof of the house and into the rainwater tank.

There is enough water in the tank for everyone who lives here.

Water from rainwater tanks is **filtered** before people drink it. This takes out any dirt from the roof.

Water for the Garden

This house has a small rainwater tank. Water from the small tank is only used in the garden.

The people who live in this house **recycle** some of their water.

Water that has been used for washing is used again. It is used to water the garden.

Water that has been used for washing people and things is called gray water.

Chapter 3

Saving Energy

We use lots of electricity in our homes.

Most electricity is made at power stations. **Air pollution** can happen when power stations make electricity.

Saving electricity helps keep the air clean.

a power station

Electricity travels from power stations to our homes through wires.

You can help save energy!

- Turn off the television when no one is watching it.
- Put on warmer clothes when it is cold instead of turning up the heat.
- Turn off lights when no one is in a room.

Energy Use

- heating and cooling
- cooking
- machines and lights
- hot water

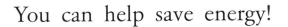

Hot Water from the Sun

Making hot water uses lots of energy.

Some homes use the heat from the sun to make hot water. Using the heat from the sun to make hot water saves a lot of energy.

This house has a hot water heater on its roof. Water goes through the heater and is warmed by the sun. Then the hot water is kept in a tank.

This kind of hot water heater is called a solar hot water heater. The word *solar* means "of the sun."

Electricity from the Sun

Some homes use **solar panels** to make electricity from the sun's light. This helps save energy.

The electricity is used to run machines inside the home.

solar panels

On sunny days, the solar panels on this house make electricity.

At night, the sun does not shine. Then the house gets electricity from a power station.

Solar panels work best in hot, sunny places.

Chapter 4

Warm Homes, Cool Homes

We use energy to keep our homes warm in winter and cool in summer.

This house has **insulation** in the walls and roof. The insulation helps keep the house warm in winter and cool in summer.

Heating and cooling use the most energy in our homes.

You can help keep your home warm in winter and cool in summer.

- Keep cold winds out of the house in winter by covering cracks under doors.

- Use blinds or shades on hot summer days to keep the house cool.

Chapter 5

Plants That Save Energy

Plants can help save energy.

In summer, these big trees help keep this house cool.

In winter, some trees have no leaves. The sun shines through the windows of the house and helps keep it warm.

Lots of plants grow on the walls of this house. The plants help keep the sun off the house walls on hot days.

Some plants need more water than others. Grow plants in your garden that don't need much water. This will help save water.

Chapter 6

Homes That Help

Homes that help save water and energy are built in many different ways.

This house has been dug into the ground. The thick earth walls help the house stay warm in winter and cool in summer.